Any time I tell people that I do triathlons, wt
love to do, I'm met with equal parts admirat
surprise. On the one hand many think that
feat, reserved only for the super athletic. Others think it's too
grueling and can't understand why someone would want to do that.
And others still view the triathlete as an endorphin-laced junky with
an unattainable degree of discipline.

Though each reaction holds its own merit, triathlon has been
deemed the fastest growing sport in the world over the last several
years and only got its start about 36 years ago.

Triathlon is a lifelong sport too: a study in the Journal of Human
Sport and Exercise suggested that experience in triathlon helped
athletes perform better and that peak age may be higher than single
endurance sports.

From my own experience, I've always noticed that I'm on the lower
end of the age spectrum. I get constant reminders throughout the
race that athletes my parents' age are perfectly suited for triathlon
competition as they steadily pass by me.

After one race I spoke with a 55 year old man who had open-heart
surgery a few years prior. He had just finished his 12th triathlon in
two years and stated that he was "obsessed". My unscientific
hypothesis is that age-related decline is not as prevalent in triathlon
since getting better requires experience: how to race, how to
transition, how to train.

Finally, as with all sports, the odds are against you competing at a
professional level. However, triathlon is great exercise, fosters a
strong community of enthusiasts, and helps to instill discipline and
mental and physical growth.

Whether your goal is to get faster, to compete in your age group, or
to find a new passion or athletic pursuit, triathlon can provide you
that platform.

I wrote this guide to bring single sport athletes into the sport of
triathlon; to encourage new athletes to join the sport; and to help
interested individuals navigate the crowded world of triathlon gear,
training, and race day nuances. The end of this guide contains
training plans for different distances and experience levels.

1) Triathlon Race Day

The most confusing thing going into my first triathlon was the concept of the transition. In short, it's your home base that you set up before the race and visit between each event. Your bike will be parked there, your gear will be set out in an orderly fashion there, you can have food and hydration there, and your shoes for the run will be there. T1 refers to the transition from swim to bike and T2 refers to the bike to run portion.

You will enter the transition area the morning of the race and it will close usually around 30 minutes to an hour before the race begins. You will set everything up and leave it there for the rest of the race, exiting transition in only your tri suit with your goggles, cap, and perhaps your wetsuit.

The Transition Station

The space where you set up your transition station is limited. Each athlete has a spot on the bike rack with their number where they will park the bike. In some races you rack your bike in the days before the race and leave it there overnight (security protected). In others, you will rack your bike in the morning.

The space under or just beside your bike is all you have, and other athletes will be setting up on either side of you. The space is about the size of a towel folded in half.

I suggest setting your transition station up on a small towel or a folded towel. In the front of the towel place your cycling shoes (or running shoes if not wearing cycling shoes).

You may choose to put your helmet upside down on top of the shoes so that you remember to put this on first. Put your sunglasses in your helmet too. I usually leave my helmet on my bike handlebars, though this is personal preference.

Behind your bike gear, put your running shoes, socks, running belt, hat, and anything else you plan to take on your run.

Depending on the length of your triathlon you need to account for nutrition and hydration. If it's an Ironman distance race you may opt to spend more time in transition to organize your nutritional needs.

However, in short races you can have this set up on the bike already and minimize time spent in transition.

Transition on Race Day
On race day it's ideal that you know your way around transition. Try to walk through the transition area during the check-in process, typically the day before the race though not always. In doing so, you can visualize your transition from swim to T1 to the bike, and your transition from bike to T2 to the run. This preparation can save you valuable time between each race leg.

As you move through the race you want to know exactly where your transition station is in relation to the racecourse. When you leave the swim you will come out of the water and jog to your station.

A useful tip is to put your helmet and sunglasses on first, buckling your helmet. Once you put your cycling shoes on, you're ready to roll.

Faster and more experienced athletes sometimes choose to have their cycling shoes clipped into their pedals already. Take your bike off the rack and run with it out of the bike exit, which will be marked, to the mount line. You can begin biking only once you are past this line.

When you finish the bike there will also be a dismount line, which you can only cross once you are off the bike. You will again run your bike through transition to your station, re-rack your bike, and take off your helmet and cycling shoes.

Strap your running belt on first so that you don't forget to have your bib number. Put your socks and shoes on, grab your hat, and start your run out of transition. You will be a bit wobbly after the bike so it may resemble a trot more than a run at first.

You will finish the race near transition and can get your belongings out of transition when the race is finished or nearly finished. Be courteous of your fellow athletes who may still be coming in and out of transition during their race.

2) Gear
Triathlon gear can be really pricey but this section was written to cover the necessities and with the price-conscious consumer in

mind. However, I've also included information about higher-end options as well as some of the superfluous gear available.

I have seen people compete in a variety of clothes, including a pro triathlete who won a race wearing only a tiny swimsuit.

At the end of the day, it comes down to comfort and price. I advocate looking for deals and buying last year's styles in most all of the suggestions that follow.

The most popular option in competition is to wear a triathlon suit, or a "tri suit". This is a singlet that you will wear for the duration of the race. It's suitable for water, has padding for the bike ride, and is breathable enough for the run. The benefits of the tri suit are:

- No need to change clothes in transition
- Sun protection
- Fast wicking
- Hydro- and aerodynamic for speed

Good tri suits average around $200, though there are many options under $100 along with very expensive options. Favorite brands at triathlons include Zoot, Roka, SLS3, Blueseventy, and Pearl Izumi.

I knew I was doing a number of triathlons in my first year and purchased the Roka Men's Elite Aero suit for $225 (less with the 15% first timer discount). It has served me very well in races from one-hour sprint triathlons to an Ironman 70.3 mile distance. It has great stretch and flexibility during the swim, is breathable during the run, and has a zip front that can provide extra breathability during the run. Some reviewers claim that the padding is not enough for cycling, but I haven't found this to be an issue.

Wattie Ink is another triathlete favorite for higher end apparel. It's easily the most eccentric of the apparel options out there thanks to ostentatious design (Captain America, skull and crossbones, etc). But reviewers praise the brand for its soft touch and all day comfort, from short distance to Ironman. Reviewers noted the brand for helping to prevent or eliminate chafing, which is a major selling point among athletes.

Leftlane Sports is my favorite spot though, with tri suit options as low as $50. You can also find good options at SwimOutlet.com and Amazon.

Finally, a sports watch is an important item. There is no question that Garmin sits atop the wearable market among athletes, though Polar, Samsung, TomTom, and Apple make popular wearables as well.

All of the newer models have GPS capability to track your watch and cycling speed and distance. If you want triathlon functionality then a Garmin or Polar is your best bet. The Garmin is especially popular as it boasts a strong bike computer capability.

You also can benefit from a watch in training as it can help you stay in targeted training intensity zones (described later) using heart rate monitor functionality and speed/pace meters.

All of the above brands feature some mix of heart rate monitoring and pace metering. However, the Apple Watch does not currently link up with a bike computer while the other brands typically have a full suite of options. The Garmins are the best but are costly, likely above $300 for everything.

Swim
You will approach the swim in your tri suit with your race-issued swim cap and goggles. You can wear more clothing and footwear if you have friends or family with you to hold onto it. However in the absence of any help, you will typically approach the swim with nothing but your cap and goggles.

Competition Gear
When purchasing goggles, you need to take into account sunlight and water transparency. If it's a sunny day in clear water, you may opt for shaded goggles. For indoor pool training, you need something lighter.

As a swimmer I have always preferred Speedo goggles. I typically train and race with the Speedo Speed Socket 2.0 mirrored goggles ($30), though if I am in a pool with lower light I will use clear goggles.

The Speed Sockets and other goggles in the Speedskin family of Speedo goggles have curved lens to increase peripheral vision. This is an especially useful feature in the triathlon when other swimmers surround you.

Tip: Avoid rubbing or touching the lens of your goggles; there is an anti-fog protectant on them.

Wetsuits are allowed when water temperatures are 78 degrees Fahrenheit or below. For swimmers, this means extra buoyancy and warmth and triathletes tend to root for wetsuit legal temperatures. If you are swimming in cold water you will certainly want a wetsuit to keep you warm. There are many types of wetsuits, and among those types, different thicknesses.

When you are searching for a wetsuit, try to find one that is specific to swimmers or triathlons. Popular brands that make these wetsuits include Roka, Xterra, Orca, Huub, and Blueseventy.

You should also consider the places you will be competing and try to research water temperatures. Based on race locations, you need to buy a wetsuit with an appropriate thickness. I suggest reading the Choosing Your Wetsuit guide by Watersports Warehouse to learn more.

Training Gear
For training purposes I swim with Speedo Sprints ($5) and use my race goggles from time to time so they don't feel totally foreign on race day. I also have a pair of Roka F2s. I like the goggles fine but prefer the comfort of Speedos.

Popular swim training gear includes a pull buoy, kick board, and swim paddles. It is likely that your pool already has this equipment, so check first. The pull buoy goes between your knees/thighs to practice swim pulls without the kick. Paddles can increase thrust, and kick boards are helpful in developing your kick.

Men and women alike should purchase performance bathing suits that are designed for swimming laps as opposed to recreational pool activity. Speedo's Performance section has bathing suits for men and women for as low as $30. I use the Flipturns Jammer because they contain the poly spandex ProLT for support and mobility, cost $40, and should last at least a year if not more.

Bike

The bike requires more gear than you you may think as you need to take into account factors such as safety, comfort, nutrition, hydration, and most importantly, speed. Since the swim offers no opportunity for hydrating or eating, you need to fuel your body while continuing to race.

First of all, you need a bike. Bikes come in many shapes and forms but the most common ones that you see for training or racing will be triathlon/time trial bikes and road bikes.

The primary difference between a tri bike and a road bike is the angle of the seat. The tube that the tri bike seat is mounted on is more upright and sits at a higher angle. The angle helps the triathlete to achieve a greater aerodynamic position while also relieving some of the stress on the quadriceps.

Whereas a cyclist is done after a ride, the triathlete must run. The tri bike helps the triathlete with efficiency and preserves your legs (to a certain degree) for the run.

Safety

The most obvious place to start with safety is your head. Many triathletes wear aero helmets, which look like a cone is coming out of the back of your head. They may save some time but are not necessary for most. As you progress though you may opt to switch to an aero helmet.

I picked up a Specialized Align helmet for $40 when I began and have ridden with it since. It's reasonably priced and high quality. For those who want a higher-end suggestion, I also have a Trek Bontrager Ballista MIPS, which has the Multi-directional Impact Protection System (MIPS) technology. According to Trek's site: "Developed by brain surgeons and scientists, MIPS helps reduce rotational forces on the brain caused by angled impacts to the head." This is a fair priced aero helmet at $199 with high-end technology.

When I first began cycling I thought that sunglasses were just for protecting eyes from the sun and did not ride with them. As I later found out, they protect your eyes from more than just the sun.

On a recent ride my front tire kicked up a small rock from the road, which hit me directly in the right lens of my sunglasses. I swore to never ride without them again.

I ride with a $19.99 pair that I picked up from CVS and they protect my eyes from the elements just fine. Cycling-specific glasses from Oakley cost around $200 (give or take) and provide an extended peripheral vision. This is useful when you are looking ahead from a tucked cycling position, though is not essential.

Comfort

Whether training or racing, having a chamois (fancy word for the pad in cycling shorts/pants) will make your ride much more enjoyable. Bike shorts/pants or bibs that extend up over your shoulders typically have a thicker, stiffer chamois in the seat as they are designed for only cycling. Tri suits and tri shorts have a thinner, more flexible chamois for brick rides or races.

Head to Leftlane Sports for last year's cycling gear at a steep discount to pick up some cycling-specific bottoms for training sessions. Tri shorts are also worth owning for brick sessions.

One of the most uncomfortable parts of cycling is the repetitive motion of inner thighs rubbing against your bike seat. This can be alleviated, at least in part, by liberally applying Body Glide, Vaseline, Chamois Butt'r, Body Alchemy, or a similar cream to the upper inner thighs.

Nutrition & Hydration

You get most of your essential nutrition and hydration while on the bike. Whatever you consume before the swim needs to be enough to get you to the bike as you aren't likely to eat or drink again until after T1.

To hold drinks you will need to buy water bottle cages for your bike. Snacks can be held in saddle bags, which typically attach behind your seat. Another option is to get a Stealth Pocket from Xlab, which velcro straps onto your top tube for easy access while riding.

Even for sprint distance triathlons it's wise to have at a minimum one bottle of water on the bike, while many athletes choose to have a water and a sports drink. Specific hydration and nutrition options are outlined later in this book.

Speed

Finally, there are a few things to help you with cycling speed. Though I am a firm believer that the cyclist is the most important determinant of cycling speed, some accessories can help you get there.

One of the most basic accessories is clipless pedals for your bike, which you actually clip into despite what the name suggests. Clipless pedals and accompanying cycling shoes essentially connect your leg to the cycle and provide for a seamless energy transfer. Cycling shoes are typically stiff and allow for maximum energy transfer while also providing support to your foot.

I use the Look Keo 2 Max Road Pedals ($70 new, I got them used on Craigslist for $50), and purchased the accompanying Look Keo grey cleats ($25). For shoes, I got a stiff sole Lake shoe from Leftlane Sports for about $40. The cleats are screwed into your shoe, and you clip that into the pedal.

Some athletes choose a tri cycling shoe, which are not very different from a typical road shoe. These usually are built with wider insertion points for your foot, a loop of fabric on the heel to help you pull the shoe on and off, and the typical foot support a cycling road shoe has. These features could be particularly useful if you have your shoes pre-clipped onto the pedals and hop onto the bike barefoot. Otherwise, they are not necessary in my view.

Training

One of the best purchases I made was buying an indoor bike trainer. This allows you to place your back tire into a stationary rack, add resistance using a resistance wheel against your back tire, and get a good training ride while watching Netflix. I purchased a used Travel Trac Comp Fluid trainer for about $60 on Craigslist.

The fluid trainer is a good option as the internal disc spins in a sealed container with fluid in it, which causes a progressive resistance as you spin faster in order to simulate a ride on the road. It's an especially useful option to have when you're short on time, when the weather is too hot or cold, rainy or snowy, or if you live in a city that isn't conducive to outdoor rides.

Another important training item on the bike is a bike computer. This can be combined with your sports watch purchase as many watches can be mounted on your handlebars.

There are also standalone cycling computer options like the Garmin 510/520 or the Wahool Elemnt Bolt, which I have. I really like the Bolt for its simple setup, bluetooth functionality, and ease of use.

Many cyclists on online forums prefer the Bolt, specifically noting that the Garmins seem to run into technological issues. Furthermore, the Bolt has a more modern interface and their app and data is top notch.

The Garmin is $299 while the Bolt is $249, giving it a slight edge for me. Finally, a verdict from Lifehacker: "The Edge 520 feels as clunky and awkward to use as that weird GPS unit still mounted in the dashboard of a 2002 Nissan.

Add in the Elemnt's regular firmware updates that come with added features, and it's pretty clear that the Elemnt has its eye on the future where the Edge 520 is still kicking and screaming in the past."

Travel
If you are doing a local triathlon you can transport your bike by putting it on a bike rack on the back of your car. If you have an SUV, you can lay the bike down on its side in the back, which is what I do.

You can also transport bikes in sedans by taking both the front and back wheels off. The back wheel takes some practice to remove and put back on, so make sure to use Youtube to learn how to do it.

If you opt for a triathlon in a location you need to fly to, you can take the bike apart and transport it in a box. There are a few options for this: buy your own hard case or soft case and take the bike apart yourself; ship with BikeFlights.com or TriBikeTransport.com; or explore other shipping options through FedEx.

Bike boxes can cost a lot if you get a new one, but I opted for a used one that cost $120 and gets the job done. Look into airline charges for bikes before selecting your flight, as they can vary greatly across airlines.

One final option is to use Spinlister, an app/website where people rent their bikes out. I've used this option when traveling but the only drawback is that you aren't likely to be able to get a full bike fitting.

Run

Purchasing gear for the run is mostly focused on making your time in T2 as efficient as possible. If you've ridden your bike in cycling shoes then you will need to change into running shoes, otherwise you already have your running shoes on from your bike and this is one less step.

I do not wear socks during cycling and if it's a short sprint triathlon or even Olympic distance, I will not wear socks during the run. For Ironman distances you'll likely want to wear socks. However this is a personal preference so try it both ways in your training and decide what works best for you.

It's essential that you choose the right shoe for you. Everyone has a different gait and it's useful for runners with specific running-related pain to have a gait analysis at a specialized running store.

In my experience, New Balance Vazee Pace 2 has been an excellent shoe with strong support while also being lightweight. For shorter races (6.2 miles and under) I typically run in Nike Streak LT3 race flats. These are very lightweight and ideal for races, but are by no means necessary.

In Transition

There are two cheap purchases to minimize your time in T2 and make your transition effort more efficient: no-tie shoelaces and a race number belt. Lock Laces are elastic, no-tie shoelaces with a slide lock. They are a one-size-fits-all option for any running shoe and require that you only slip your shoe on, tighten the lock, and go. These cost under $10 or you can get a pack of three for around $20 on Amazon.

Athletes must wear a paper bib with their race number during the run. The first time I did a triathlon I spent several minutes in T2 pinning my number to my tri suit with safety pins. I watched a guy who came intro transition at the same time I did slip his belt on leave a full minute before me.

You can avoid this with a race number belt that you can clip your number into the night before and then buckle on. These also have additional loops if you decide to take along snacks or water bottles. I went with the X31 belt for $10 and have been perfectly happy with it.

Other Accessories
I typically run with a hat, both for sun protection and to minimize sweat dripping in my eyes. Some prefer sunglasses, while others are fine without anything.

Depending on the distance of your run you may also want to take handheld running water bottles or snacks and nutrition. I am fine with the drink and snack stations along the run and leave my own nutrition or hydration behind.

Note that music and headphones are not allowed in the triathlon so plan on leaving that behind. I've included a day-of-the-race checklist at the end of this book.

Recovery Gear
Finally, triathlon training requires that you take care of your body by way stretching, a sensible training plan, and rest. This can be free, but there is some gear that you may choose to purchase to aid you in the recovery process.

Aside from stretching, a foam roller can be your best friend, helping you through recovery while preventing injuries. Though there isn't conclusive scientific research on benefits, foam rolling works similar to a deep tissue massage. It is believed to increase muscle range of motion (in the short term) and help with soreness. It's important to continue to stay limber and loose, and adding stretching after any workout as well as on off days is a good habit to develop.

Recovery also consists of rest when needed. Many athletes push through pain without listening to the signals their body is giving them. This is typically a mistake that only exacerbates an issue. I've learned that taking extra time to rest an injury allows you to get back to training efficiently as opposed to letting the injury ripen into something that keeps you out an extended time.

VooDoo Floss Bands are a good option for targeting specific injured areas. These are large, thick bands of rubber that are wrapped tightly around your knee, ankle, thigh, or other injured area. These are worn for just a few minutes at a time and work to slow circulation and then provide a rush of blood to the area when removed.

According to Rogue Fitness, "the resulting compression and "flossing" of activated muscles can help reduce swelling, re-perfuse stiff connective tissues, restore joint mechanics, and encourage swifter recovery and overall flexibility." I've used the bands for knee and ankle pain and they helped me through recovery.

Another simple option for targeting tight muscles is a lacrosse ball. It functions similarly to a foam roller but is generally harder and can be used to get into smaller areas in the back and legs. It's also more travel-friendly than a foam roller.

During the lead-up to my Ironman 70.3 race I discovered the magic of a simple bath. Some athletes like to add Epsom salt to their baths, which is said to help with arthritis, soreness, and a host of other issues, though this is not supported by science. It can be scented and make the water feel silky, which could also be an appealing aspect, but in any case warm baths allow you to submerge your legs to loosen joints and relax muscles.

Winter Gear
Finally, all of the gear above needs to be adjusted by season. In the winter you can still bike and run outdoors, but you need to wear gear tailored to the weather.

Cycling in the cold is more uncomfortable than running due to the speed of the bike. It is essential to get windproof cycling gloves since your hands are out in front on the handlebars.

You will also benefit from a windproof vest or jacket to help keep your core warm. Castelli has high-end cycling gear which I particularly like for cold weather. As usual, look first on Leftlane for good deals on Castelli gear. I also like the cold weather gear from De Soto, an outfitter with gear for covering you from head to toe.

You will need to experiment with what to wear on a cold weather run. You will warm up quickly and may find that certain gloves or jackets are overkill for cold weather running. I run in Pearl Izumi running tights and Nike Running tights. Note that these tights are different than "training" tights, which are designed gym work and not running.

I also recommend a thermal top from De Soto or a Nike Running shirt or jacket, both with thumb holes to pull the sleeve over your hands. In cold or windy weather you may also want an ear warmer band, which can be picked up for very cheap on Amazon.

List 1 - Essentials
Tri-suit
Running shoes
Water and hydration
Nutrition

List 2 - Race Day Checklist
Swim
Tri suit
Goggles
Cap
Ankle timing chip

Bike
Helmet
Sunglasses
Shoes
Snacks for your bike
Flat kit

Run
Shoes
Hat
Watch
Race belt

3) Training

Preparation for a triathlon typically refers to a combination of endurance and speed training. Most coaches have their own take on the subject but nobody will disagree that you need a solid endurance base.

You may be able to swim 500 meters, or bike 11 miles, or run a 5K, but can you do them in succession? Building a solid base will allow you to train more effectively.

When I began triathlon training I was barely able to run two miles without stopping. Others come into training as an already-established swimmer/cyclist/runner.

You need to assess where you stand with regards to endurance as well as in each discipline. This assessment is more art than science, but see how far you are able to go in each discipline to gauge your fitness level.

You also need to appreciate the difference between being in shape at only one of the sports versus being in triathlon shape. A high level of cardio from running is a great start, but doesn't mean your upper body muscles or breathing techniques are sufficient for a distance swim. Likewise, being in great swimming shape does not translate to leg muscle strength for a bike ride that then feeds into a run.

Prior to beginning training I found it was useful to go on several short runs and swim as many laps as I could on several occasions. I also took some indoor cycling classes to help get my legs under me and get my body accustomed to several motions across the three sports in a given week.

It's more of an art than a science as you start to get into shape, but spend at least three weeks (preferably more) slowly building up to beginning a training regimen. Finally, triathlon is supposed to be fun so if you haven't trained or are going into a race with minimal training, you may suffer and miss out on the enjoyable parts of the race.

Distance
It's hard to recommend that you do a certain distance triathlon, but you likely want to test it out with some shorter races to begin with. There's no replacement for race pace and competition, and learning how to move from swim to bike to run can only be accomplished by experience.

Athletes that already have experience in endurance running or cycling may even jump right to Olympic distance triathlons. However, if you choose Ironman distance races you start to need more training and race equipment, and need to learn a lot about the specifics of endurance training and race strategy as well as nutrition. Some say that at that distance it's more about execution than speed or fitness.

As you would expect, training volume and mileage is significantly higher as you train for longer races. There are certainly many high intensity methods that could benefit the triathlete, but an endurance base can't be achieved without some volume.

Intensity
The intensity with which you train varies from athlete to athlete and is largely based on the goals of the individual: to finish, to race, to place, to win. Triathlon training typically takes place in Zones 1-5, which refer to both heart rate (summarized in the table below) and pace (athlete specific). A training plan will say something like "Run 30 minutes in Zone 2", so you will adjust your effort for that run to match Zone 2.

I trained for my first triathlon without paying close attention to training zones, but rather using the zone descriptions below (easy to very hard). This is not necessarily an advisable tactic, but it did work for me at that time. Since then, I try to stick with target heart rate zones because they help you progress in specific ways.

Zone & Description	Target Heart Rate (% of max)
Zone 1 - Recovery - Easy	55-70
Zone 2 - Endurance - Steady	70-75
Zone 3 - Tempo - Comfortable	75-80
Zone 4 - Threshold - Uncomfortable	80-88
Zone 5 - VO2 Max - Hard to very hard	80-88

The first question you probably have is what your max heart rate is. The Mayo Clinic states that your maximum heart rate should be equal to 220 minus your age.

Example: If you're 25 your maximum heart rate should be 195. You should then adjust your efforts in training to keep your heart rate in the target zone outlined above. If you do a 30 minute run in Zone 2, your heart rate should be around 136-146.

If you are interested in setting power zones as well, which take into account pace and power, I recommend accessing Joe Friel's Quick Guide to Setting Zones. This can be found free on TrainingPeaks.com.

Plans
I have included training plans here for a sprint triathlon and an Olympic triathlon. There are some events that are only barely less than an Olympic; for those I suggest using the Olympic plan. These can be found in the appendix at the end of the book.

In addition to the training plans I also suggest taking yoga or Pilates once a week. You may also choose to implement some weight lifting into your routine. I regret not doing so when I first started training and think that I could benefit from strength training, essentially generating more power. Most any coach will support strength training as a part of your regimen and scientific research supports this as well.

4) Nutrition & Hydration
Eating and drinking during a triathlon provide you with the energy to finish the race and keep you healthy to finish the race. If it's a short sprint triathlon (total of around 14-15 miles), you could likely get by just with water bottles stored on your bike. However, longer races require that you plan ahead, eating on the bike to begin digesting foods that provide you with energy to finish the race strong.

For a long race you typically need to ingest 40-50g of carbohydrates and around 400 calories each hour of the bike. I avoid all energy gels (Clif, Gu, Hammer, etc) as they have maltodextrin and fructose and since they are designed to be consumed with vast quantities of water.

During a race you begin to get dehydrated. When the concentrated carbohydrates from a gel are put into a dehydrated gut your body essentially channels water to help with the digestion, making you more dehydrated.

I prefer Skratch energy chews as you can take them every few minutes rather than all at once like a gel. Each drop has 16 calories and 4g of carbohydrates, and tastes good too.

Hydrating and nutrition are not mutually exclusive since you can achieve your calorie and carbohydrate goals with the sports drink. Try to use this to your advantage when planning out race nutrition.

Similarly, you want to hydrate with water and a sports drink. I prefer to use Osmo Active Hydration (separate formulas for women and men). I choose Osmo Active Hydration for in-race hydration as it it's been formulated with glucose, sucrose, electrolytes, and carbohydrates to restore hydration and power output. It's also a product that's been developed with peer-reviewed scientific findings that support its ingredients and the effects.

Osmo states that when you're thirsty, your body water is already around 2% below optimal levels which can result in 11% reduced power output. Osmo is the fastest way to replenish body water and also gives you an additional ~90 calories and 22.5g of carbohydrates as well as the electrolytes you need as you get dehydrated.

Nuun is a popular tablet for hydration as well but has a carbonated effect that is not comfortable during activity.

For nutrition, you will need to experiment to see what works best for you. Some triathletes eat sandwiches or peanut butter wraps during rides. Others opt for energy gels, chews, honey, or activity waffles. I am very careful about what I choose from the latter group as they contain maltodextrin and fructose, which can cause gastrointestinal discomfort. For most gels and chews it's near impossible to consume them with sufficient water, further contributing to issues in the gut.

My favorite snacks are Skratch Fruit Chews ($24 for 10 packs, low fructose), sandwich with deli meat (I've only tried this on training rides), Mojo bars (no fructose), or Luna bars (no wax coating, no nuts). You should start off with solids and work your way to liquid while on the bike. However during a short triathlon you may not be on the bike for more than 20 minutes, in which case water and a sports drink are sufficient.

The three plans below will prepare you for a sprint or olympic distance triathlon. Missing a day is not the end of the world, but I suggest sticking to the plan as closely as possible.

Use the training zones above to help you know how much effort to put into your workout. The zones are denoted by Z1, Z2, etc. The swim workouts are grouped into multiples of 50.

Swimming sets are grouped by their lap count: one lap in a pool is 25 yards or meters, unless you are in an olympic pool, which is usually 50 meters. Thus, 50 is two laps and 100 is four laps. If you see 4x100, then that is four sets of four laps.

Brick workouts refer to bike straight into run, which simulates race day. You should try to start your run within 1-2 minutes from your bike ride to get used to that.

Plan 1 - Sprint

Week 1

Monday	Rest	
Tuesday	Bike	30 minutes Z1
Wednesday	Run	20 minutes Z1-Z2
Thursday	Bike	Warmup 100, 4x100 Z1 with 1 minute rest
Friday	Rest	
Saturday	Bike	45 minutes Z1
Sunday	Run	20 minutes Z1

Week 2

Monday	Rest	
Tuesday	Bike	40 minutes Z1
Wednesday	Run	20 minutes Z1-Z2

Thursday	Bike	Warmup 100, 5x100 Z1 with 1 minute rest
Friday	Rest	
Saturday	Bike	50 minutes Z1
Sunday	Swim	Warmup 100, 2x200 Z1 with 1 minute rest, 50 cool down

Week 3

Monday	Rest	
Tuesday	Bike	35 minutes Z1
Wednesday	Run	20 minutes Z1-Z2
Thursday	Swim	Warmup 100, 3x200, 100 cool down
Friday	Strength	
Saturday	Bike	60 minutes Z1
Sunday	Run + Swim	30 minutes run Z1, 10 minute continuous swim Z1, 4x50 Z4 with 45 second rest, 50 cool down

Week 4

Monday	Rest	
Tuesday	Bike	30 minutes Z2
Wednesday	Run	20 minutes Z1-Z2
Thursday	Bike	30 minutes Z1
Friday	Rest	
Saturday	Bike	45 minutes Z1

Sunday	Run + Swim	30 minutes run Z1, 3x300 Z1 with 1 minute rest

Week 5

Monday	Rest	
Tuesday	Brick	Bike 30 minutes Z1 into 10 minutes Z1 run
Wednesday	Run	20 minutes Z1 with 30 second hard efforts after minutes 8 and 15
Thursday	Swim	200 warmup, 4x200 Z1 with 45 second rest, cool down your choice
Friday	Rest	
Saturday	Bike	70 minutes Z1
Sunday	Swim	100 warmup, 2x500 easy

Week 6

Monday	Rest	
Tuesday	Brick	Bike 35 minutes Z1 into 15 minutes Z1 run
Wednesday	Run	20 minutes Z1
Thursday	Swim	800 easy, 100 easy cool down
Friday	Strength	
Saturday	Bike	75 minutes Z1
Sunday	Run + Swim	Run 45 minutes Z1, Swim 900 continuous

Week 7

Monday	Rest	
Tuesday	Brick	Bike 40 minutes Z1 into 15 minutes Z1 run
Wednesday	Run	20 minutes Z1 with 30 second hard efforts after minutes 8 and 15
Thursday	Swim	200 warmup, 4x500 Z1 with 45 second rest, cool down your choice
Friday	Rest	
Saturday	Bike	50 minutes Z1
Sunday	Swim	800 easy with short cool down

Week 8

Monday	Rest	
Tuesday	Bike	30 minutes Z1
Wednesday	Run	20 minutes Z1
Thursday	Swim	4x100 Z4, 200 easy
Friday	Rest	
Saturday	Bike + Swim	Bike 10 minutes easy with fast legs, Swim 400
Sunday	Race day!	

Plans 2 & 3 - Olympic
These plans are 10 weeks in length aimed towards establishing an endurance base and then tailored to getting faster and better. The easy plan is for those who are more interested in just finishing the race, while the advanced plan will help you to kick your training into a higher gear. They are very similar, but the first has been smoothed over for less experienced athletes. I used Plan 3 (Advanced) for my first race and felt very well prepared.

Each plan assumes that you've been training for a few weeks already with some swims, bikes, and runs. These should start slow and short in distance if you haven't been training. They will help you to get your legs under you and get your body used to bringing the disciplines together in a single week.

For the pre-training sessions I recommend swimming laps until you need a break, and just getting these laps in at a slow and steady pace. Cycling sessions can be easy and relaxed, going for 45 minutes to an hour to get your legs used to spinning. Indoor cycling classes are also a good option. Finally, I recommend runs of 20, 20, and 30 minutes, if possible, also at an easy pace.

Plan 2 - Olympic - Easy

Week 1

Monday	Rest	
Tuesday	Swim	Warmup 200 easy, 4x100 Z3 with 15 second rest, 150 cool down easy
Wednesday	Run	20 minutes Z1-Z2
Thursday	Bike	15 miles Z2
Friday	Run	25 minutes Z1
Saturday	Swim	Warmup 200 easy, 8x50 Z4 with 10 second rest, 150 cool down easy
Sunday	Bike	20 Miles Z1

Week 2

Monday	Rest	
Tuesday	Swim	Warmup 200 easy, 4x100 Z2 with 15 second rest, 150 cooldown easy
Wednesday	Bike	15 miles Z2
Thursday	Run	25 minutes Z1-Z2

Friday	Brick	10 mile bike followed immediately by 15 minute easy run
Saturday	Swim + Run	300 warmup, 5x100 Z1/Z2 with 15 second rest, 200 cooldown
Sunday	Bike	25 Miles Z1

Week 3

Monday	Rest	
Tuesday	Swim	Warmup 300 easy, 8x100 Z3 with 30 second rest, 150 cooldown easy
Wednesday	Bike	20 miles Z1
Thursday	Run	30 minutes Z1-Z2
Friday	Brick	15 mile bike
Saturday	Swim	Warmup 250 easy, 4x200, breathing every 3, 5, 7 strokes on sets 1 and 3, easy swim on sets 2 and 4.
Sunday	Bike	30 Miles: 20 minute warm up Z1 with 5x10-second surges to Z5, then rest of time Z1

Week 4

Monday	Rest	
Tuesday	Swim	Warmup 200 easy, then 3x400 easy
Wednesday	Bike	15 miles Z1
Thursday	Run	20 minutes Z1-Z2
Friday	Rest	
Saturday	Swim	Warmup 300 easy, 8x50 hard with 30 second rest, 100 cooldown easy

Sunday	Bike	20 miles Z1

Week 5

Monday	Swim	Warmup 300 easy, 6x50 faster each 50 with 15 second rest, 100 backstroke Z1, 4x50 pull Z4 with 30 second rest, 100 breast Z1, 4x50 Z4 with 30 second rest
Tuesday	Run	Warmup 10 minutes Z2, 5 minutes in Z3, 3 minutes Z2, 3 sets of 3 min in Z4 with 2 minutes in Z1 recovery, cool down 10 minutes Z2.
Wednesday	Brick	Bike 1 hour 30 minutes in Z2 into run 10 minutes in Z2
Thursday	Swim	200 warmup easy, 2x200 freestyle Z2 with 10 seconds rests, 100 kick Z2, 3x150 pull Z3 with 15 second rests, 100 kick Z2, 4x100 freestyle Z4 with 30 second rests
Friday	Rest	
Saturday	Bike	Warmup 30 minutes in Z2, 4x30 seconds in Z5 with 90 second recoveries in Z1, 3x9 minutes in Z4 with 5 minute recoveries in Z1, Cooldown 30 minutes in Z2
Sunday	Run	45 minutes in Z2 - Z3, preferably on soft surface with some hills

Week 6

Monday	Swim	Warmup 350 easy, 4x100 faster with each set rest 30-45 seconds, 100 backstroke Z1, 4x100 pull faster each set rest 30 seconds, 100 breaststroke Z1, 4x100 freestyle Z4 rest 30 seconds, 100 cooldown
Tuesday	Run	Warmup 10 minutes in Z2, 5 minutes in

		Z3, 3 minutes in Z2, 3x4 minutes in Z4 with 3 minutes Z1 recoveries, cooldown 5mins in Z2
Wednesday	Brick	Bike 1 hour 15 minutes in Z2, run 10 minutes in Z2
Thursday	Swim	Warmup 400, 300 freestyle Z2 rest 40 seconds, 300 pull Z3 rest 30 seconds, 200 kick Z4 rest 20 seconds, 100 freestyle Z4, Slow 100 cooldown
Friday	Rest	Stretch
Saturday	Bike	Warmup 30 minutes in Z2, 4x30 seconds in Z5 with 1min 30 seconds recoveries in Z1, 2x15 minutes in Z3 with 5 minute recoveries in Z1 Cooldown 30 minutes in Z2
Sunday	Run	1 hour in Z2 - Z3, preferably on soft surface with some hills

Week 7

Monday	Swim	Warmup choice, 2x200 freestyle Z3 with 45 second rests, 100 kick Z2, 2x100 pull Z3 with 45 second rests, 100 kick Z2, 4x100 freestyle Z4 with 45 second rests
Tuesday	Run	Warmup 10 minutes in Z2 5 minutes in Z3, 3 minutes in Z2, 3x5 minutes in Z4 with 3 minutes Z1 recoveries Cooldown 5mins in Z2
Wednesday	Brick	Bike 1 hour 15 minutes in Z2 into run 10 minutes as 3 minutes in Z4, 7 minutes in Z1
Thursday	Swim	Warmup 400 slow, 100 kick Z2, 200 freestyle, 300 pull, 400 freestyle, 300 pull, 200 freestyle, 100 kick all in Z2 with 15

		seconds rest
Friday	Rest	
Saturday	Bike	Bike 25 miles into run 6.2 miles, all in Z2
Sunday	Run	30 minutes open water in Z2

Week 8

Monday	Swim	Warmup 200 easy, 300 pull Z2 rest 30 seconds, 400 freestyle Z4, 400 pull Z2 rest 30 seconds, 400 freestyle Z4
Tuesday	Run	Warmup 10 minutes in Z2, 5 minutes as (20 seconds Z5, 40 seconds Z1), 2x10 minutes in Z4 with 5 minutes in Z1, 5 minute cooldown in Z2
Wednesday	Brick	Bike 1 hour 30 minutes in Z2 into run 10 minutes as 5 minutes in Z4, 5 minutes in Z1
Thursday	Swim	Warmup choice, 300 as (25 kick, 50 freestyle) Z3 with 30 second rests, 200 as (50 BACK/50 breast) Z2 with 30 second rests, 300 pull Z3 with 30 second rests, 200 kick Z2 with 30 second rests, 300 freestyle Z2 with 30 second rests
Friday	Rest	Stretch or mobility training
Saturday	Bike	Warmup 20 minutes Z2, 5x(30 seconds Z5, 30 seconds Z1) hour time trial in upper Z3 to Z4 into run 10 minutes as 4 minutes Z4, 6 minutes Z1
Sunday	Run	Run for 50 minutes on hilly ground, off road, in Z2

Week 9

Monday	Swim	Warmup choice, 700 freestyle Z3 with 60 second rest, 100 kick Z2, 400 pull Z4

Tuesday	Run	Warmup 10 minutes in Z2, 5 minutes as 20 seconds Z5, 40 seconds Z1, 7x1 minute in Z4/Z5 with 3 minutes in Z1, Cooldown 5 minutes in Z2
Wednesday	Brick	Bike 1 hour 30 minutes in Z2 into run 10 minutes as 5 minutes in Z4, 5 minutes in Z1
Thursday	Swim	Warmup choice, 500 freestyle Z3, 500 pull Z3, 500 freestyle Z3 with 60 second rests
Friday	Rest	
Saturday	Bike	Warmup 30 minutes Z2, 5x(30 seconds Z5, 30 seconds Z1) 30 minutes time trial in Z4 into run 10 minutes as 5 minutes Z4, 5 minutes Z1
Sunday	Run	Run for 40 minutes on hilly ground, off road, in Z2

Week 10

Monday	Swim	Short easy warmup, 5x100 freestyle in Z4 with 30 seconds rest
Tuesday	Run	Warmup 10 minutes in Z2, 5mins as (20 seconds Z5, 40 seconds Z1) 7x1min in Z4/Z5 with 3 minutes in Z1 Cooldown 5 minutes in Z2
Wednesday	Brick	
Thursday	Swim	Short easy warmup, 2x200 freestyle in Z4 with 30 seconds (pool or open water)
Friday	Bike	Warmup 30 minutes in Z2, 10 minutes in Z3 Cool down 20 minutes in Z2
Saturday	Bike	Spin your legs for a half hour, easy just to stay loose

Sunday	Race Day!	

Plan 3 - Olympic - Advanced

Week 1

Monday	Rest	
Tuesday	Swim	Warmup 200 easy, 4x100 Z3 with 15 second rest, 150 cool down easy
Wednesday	Run	20 minutes Z1-Z2
Thursday	Bike	15 miles Z2
Friday	Run	25 minutes Z1
Saturday	Swim	Warmup 200 easy, 8x50 Z4 with 10 second rest, 150 cool down easy
Sunday	Bike	20 Miles Z1

Week 2

Monday	Rest	
Tuesday	Swim	Warmup 200 easy, 4x100 Z2 with 15 second rest, 150 cooldown easy
Wednesday	Bike	15 miles Z2
Thursday	Run	25 minutes Z1-Z2
Friday	Brick	10 mile bike followed immediately by 15 minute easy run
Saturday	Swim + Run	300 warmup, 5x100 Z1/Z2 with 15 second rest, 200 cooldown Run: 20 minutes Z1

Sunday	Bike	25 Miles Z1

Week 3

Monday	Rest	
Tuesday	Swim	Warmup 300 easy, 8x100 Z3 with 30 second rest, 150 cooldown easy
Wednesday	Bike	20 miles Z1
Thursday	Run	30 minutes Z1-Z2
Friday	Brick	15 mile bike followed by easy 15 minute run
Saturday	Swim	Warmup 250 easy, 4x200, breathing every 3, 5, 7 strokes on sets 1 and 3, easy swim on sets 2 and 4.
Sunday	Bike	30 Miles: 20 minute warm up Z1 with 5 10-second surges to Z5, then rest of time Z1

Week 4

Monday	Rest	
Tuesday	Swim	Warmup 200 easy, then 3x500 easy
Wednesday	Bike	15 miles Z1
Thursday	Run	20 minutes Z1-Z2
Friday	Rest	
Saturday	Swim	Warmup 300 easy, 10x50 hard with 15 second rest, 200 cooldown easy
Sunday	Bike	20 miles Z1

Week 5

Monday	Swim	Warmup 300, 8x50 faster each 50 with 15 second rest, 100 backstroke Z1, 6x50 pull Z4 with 30 second rest, 100 breast Z1, 4x50 Z4 with 30 second rest
Tuesday	Run	Warmup 10 minutes Z2, 5 minutes in Z3, 3 minutes Z2, 5 sets of 3 min in Z4 with 2 minutes in Z1 recovery, cool down 10 minutes Z2.
Wednesday	Brick	Bike hour 30 minutes in Z2 into run 10 minutes in Z2
Thursday	Swim	200 Warmup, 2x200 freestyle Z2 with 10 seconds rests, 100 kick Z2, 3x150 pull Z3 with 15s seconds, 100 kick Z2, 4x100 freestyle Z4 with 30 seconds
Friday	Rest	
Saturday	Bike	Warmup 30 minutes in Z2, 4x30 seconds in Z5 with 90 seconds recoveries in Z1 3x9mins in Z4 with 5mins recoveries in Z1, Cooldown 30 minutes in Z2
Sunday	Run	1 hour in Z2 - Z3, preferably on soft surface with some hills

Week 6

Monday	Swim	Warmup 350, 4x100 faster with each set rest 30-45 seconds, 100 backstroke Z1, 4x100 pull faster each set rest 30 seconds, 100 breaststroke Z1, 4x100 freestyle Z4 rest 30 seconds, 100 cooldown
Tuesday	Run	Warmup 10 minutes in Z2, 5mins in Z3, 3 minutes in Z2, 4x4 minutes in Z4 with 3 minute Z1 recoveries, cooldown 5 minutes in Z2

Wednesday	Brick	Bike 1 hour 30 minutes in Z2, run 10 minutes in Z2
Thursday	Swim	Warmup 400, 400 freestyle Z2 rest 40 seconds, 300 pull Z3 rest 30 seconds, 200 kick Z4 rest 20 seconds, 100 freestyle Z4, Slow 100 cooldown
Friday	Rest	Stretch
Saturday	Bike	Warmup 30 minutes in Z2, 4x30 seconds in Z5 with 1 minute 30 seconds recoveries in Z1, 2x15 minutes in Z4 with 5 minutes recoveries in Z1, Cooldown 30 minutes in Z2
Sunday	Run	1 hour in Z2 - Z3, preferably on soft surface with some hills

Week 7

Monday	Swim	Warmup choice, 2x200 freestyle Z3 with 45 second rests, 100 kick Z2, 2x200 pull Z3 with 45 second rests, 100 kick Z2, 4x100 freestyle Z4 45 second rests
Tuesday	Run	Warmup 10 minutes in Z2 5 minutes in Z3, 3 minutes in Z2, 3x5 minutes in Z4 with 3 minutes Z1 recoveries, Cooldown 5 minutes in Z2
Wednesday	Brick	Bike hour 30 minutes in Z2 into run 10 minutes as (5 minutes in Z4, 5 minutes in Z1)
Thursday	Swim	Warmup 400 slow, 100 kick Z2, 200 freestyle, 300 pull, 400 freestyle, 300 pull, 200 freestyle, 100 kick all in Z2 with 15s seconds rest
Friday	Rest	
Saturday	Bike	Bike 25 miles into run 6.2 miles, all in Z2

Sunday	Run	30 minutes, open water in Z2

Week 8

Monday	Swim	Warmup 300 slow, 400 pull Z2 rest 30 seconds, 400 freestyle Z4, 400 pull Z2 rest 30 seconds, 400 freestyle Z4
Tuesday	Run	Warmup 10 minutes in Z2, 5mins as (20 seconds Z5, 40 seconds Z1) 2x10 minutes in Z4 with 5 minutes in Z1, Cool down 5 minutes in Z2
Wednesday	Brick	Bike 1 hour 30 minutes in Z2 into run 10 minutes as 5 minutes in Z4, 5 minutes in Z1
Thursday	Swim	Warmup choice, 300 as (25 kick, 50 freestyle) Z3 with 30 seconds rest, 200 as (50 back/50 breast) Z2 with 30 second rest, 300 pull Z3 with 30 second rest, 200 kick Z2 with 30 second rest, 300 freestyle Z2 with 30 second rest
Friday	Rest	Stretch or mobility training
Saturday	Bike	Warmup 20 minutes Z2, 5x(30 seconds Z5, 30 seconds Z1) 1 hour TT in upper Z3 to Z4 into run 10 minutes as 5 minutes Z4, 5 minutes Z1
Sunday	Run	Run for 50 minutes on hilly ground, off road, in Z2

Week 9

Monday	Swim	Warmup choice, 800 freestyle Z3 with 60 second rest, 100 kick Z2, 600 pull Z4
Tuesday	Run	Warmup 10 minutes in Z2, 5mins as (20 seconds Z5, 40 seconds Z1) 7x1 minute in Z4/Z5 with 3 minutes in Z1, Cooldown 5 minutes in Z2

Wednesday	Brick	Bike 1 hour 30 minutes in Z2 into run 10 minutes as 5 minutes in Z4, 5 minutes in Z1
Thursday	Swim	Warmup choice, 500 freestyle Z3, 500 pull Z3, 500 freestyle Z3 with 60 second rests
Friday	Rest	
Saturday	Bike	Warmup 30 minutes Z2, 5x(30 seconds Z5, 30 seconds Z1), 30 minutes TT in Z4 into run 10 minutes as 5 minutes Z4, 5minutes Z1
Sunday	Run	Run for 40 minutes on hilly ground, off road, in Z2

Week 10

Monday	Swim	Short easy warmup, 5x100 freestyle in Z4 with 30 seconds rest
Tuesday	Run	Warmup 10 minutes in Z2, 5mins as (20 seconds Z5, 40 seconds Z1) 7x1min in Z4/Z5 with 3 minutes in Z1, Cooldown 5 minutes in Z2
Wednesday	Brick	
Thursday	Swim	Short easy warmup, 2x200 freestyle in Z4 with 30 second rests (pool or open water)
Friday	Bike	Warmup 30 minutes in Z2, 10 minutes in Z3, Cool down 20 minutes in Z2
Saturday	Bike	Spin your legs for a half hour, easy just to stay loose
Sunday	Race Day!	

Printed in Great Britain
by Amazon